LOVE
LETTERS

Deborah Brown

for mikey

with

LOVE

LOVE
LETTERS

Deborah Brown

O and **L** first met

in a crowded room.

L "

Although initially they were drawn together

"

they found they were both left speechless.

L tried to be a bit **bolder**

but that just left **O** feeling faint.

L sent **O** an awkward text

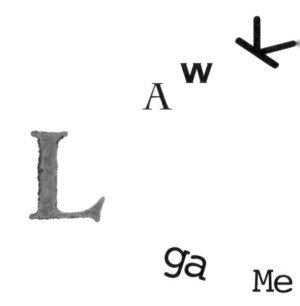

A **w** k

L

ga

Me

They just never seemed

O replied with mixed messages.

sses

quite on the same page.

That might have been it if their
friends **M** and **N** hadn't intervened.

L^M ⟷ $_N$O

They encouraged them to try one more time.

And finally you couldn't shut them up.

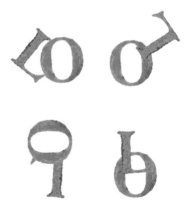

It was all **L–O–L–O**

... hello.

They wasted no time and
married in a shower of kisses.

L had been told this might happen but was still surprised by how much **O**'s character changed.

LO
L O
L

It wasn't just her size but
her colouring looked a bit off.

Then one day all was explained
and out popped little **e.**

LOᵥℯ

And not long after, wee **v.**

V and **E** grew and grew.

All was good,

except **O** seemed sad...

LOvE

... distracted even.

Torn in two,

O didn't know which way to turn.

Who left who?

It was hard to tell.

L and **O** sought support.

S

O J

VE

With help they learned to communicate better and finally seemed to make sense as a family.

By then though **E** was fully grown
and was the first to go.

LOV

With **V**, as ever, not so far behind.

Left alone they found that they fitted well together.

But then one day with **O** watching,
L slipped quietly and gently away.

First published in 2019
by Hikari Press, London

www.hikaripress.co.uk

Distributed in the UK by
Combined Book Services Limited
Paddock Wood Distribution Centre
Paddock Wood
Tonbridge
Kent TN12 6UU
www.combook.co.uk

ISBN: 978-0-9956478-3-1

Hikari Press gratefully acknowledges the financial support of Arts Council
England through Grants for the Arts.

British Library Cataloguing-in-Publication-Data.
A catalogue record of the book is available from the British Library.

Printed in England by Gomer Press

There are many people I wish to thank for this book, starting with my publisher Isabel Brittain and our mutual friend Gilly Blease. Without their faith, support and understanding I know this book wouldn't exist.

I also owe a huge debt to my tutors and fellow students on the MA in Illustration at Anglia Ruskin. They opened my mind to the infinite possibilities of what an illustrated book can be.

And finally my husband Michael and my not-so-baby boys, Solomon and Ezra, for whom love is an endlessly complicated yet beautiful four-letter word.

LOVE